# LEGO® STAR WARS™

# THE FORCE AWAKENS

Written by David Fentiman

Penguin
Random
House

**Written and Edited by** David Fentiman
**Senior Designer** Owen Bennett
**Pre-Production Producer** Marc Staples
**Senior Producer** Lloyd Robertson
**Managing Editor** Paula Regan
**Managing Art Editor** Guy Harvey
**Art Director** Lisa Lanzarini
**Publisher** Julie Ferris
**Publishing Director** Simon Beecroft

Dorling Kindersley would like to thank Randi Sørensen, Paul Hansford, and Martin Leighton Lindhardt at the LEGO Group.

**For Lucasfilm**
**Senior Editor** Jennifer Heddle
**Art Director** Troy Alders
**Story Group** Leland Chee, Pablo Hidalgo, and Rayne Roberts

First American Edition, 2016
Published in the United States by DK Publishing
345 Hudson Street, New York, New York 10014

Page design copyright © 2016 Dorling Kindersley Limited
DK, a Division of Penguin Random House LLC
16 17 18 19 20  10 9 8 7 6 5 4 3 2 1
001–280550–March/16

A catalog record for this book is available from the Library of Congress.

ISBN 978-1-4654-3818-8 (Hardback)
ISBN 978-1-4654-3819-5 (Paperback)

DK books are available at special discounts when purchased in bulk for sales promotions,
premiums, fund-raising, or educational use. For details, contact: DK Publishing Special
Markets, 345 Hudson Street, New York, New York 10014
SpecialSales@dk.com

Printed and bound in the USA

www.LEGO.com
www.starwars.com
www.dk.com

A WORLD OF IDEAS:
SEE ALL THERE IS TO KNOW

2

# Contents

# The First Order

Many years ago, the evil Empire ruled the galaxy. The Empire was harsh and cruel, and the people of the galaxy wanted to be free.

A brave rebellion began. After many hard battles, the rebels freed the galaxy!

The rebels didn't know that some members of the Empire had escaped. These Imperials traveled to the far side of the galaxy and named themselves the First Order.

Ever since then, the First Order has been planning its revenge.

# First Order commanders

Supreme Leader Snoke is in charge of the First Order. Snoke is very mysterious and keeps himself hidden. He relies on three commanders who control the First Order for him.

**Kylo Ren** is the greatest warrior in the First Order. He uses a lightsaber to defeat his enemies.

**General Hux** is very smart.
He is in charge of the
First Order's army.
Hux is building the
First Order's new secret
weapon, the Starkiller.

**Captain Phasma**
leads the First Order's
soldiers, known as
stormtroopers.
She is brave
in battle,
but cruel.

# The Resistance

Princess Leia was one of the rebels who defeated the Empire. She never believed that the Empire was gone forever.

Leia created a group called the Resistance, who would watch for signs that evil had returned.

Many brave pilots and soldiers
have joined the Resistance.
They want to protect the galaxy.

The Resistance has built a
secret base where its members
spy on the First Order.
Leia wants to know what the
First Order is planning to do.

# The village

Poe Dameron is Leia's
best pilot. Leia gives Poe a
top-secret mission. He must
fly to the planet Jakku and
meet an adventurer named
Lor San Tekka. Lor has
secret information that
can help the Resistance.

Poe lands on Jakku with
his loyal droid, BB-8.
Jakku is a hot, dry desert.
It is not a place where most
people would want to live.

Lor San Tekka lives in a village in the wilderness. Poe finds him, and Lor gives Poe a special object. The object has the information hidden inside it.

# Invasion

The First Order has attacked Jakku! Stormtoopers have come to the village looking for Lor San Tekka and his secret object.

The villagers try to fight, but there are too many stormtroopers! They have to surrender.

Poe gives the object to BB-8.
The little droid manages to
get away, but Poe is captured.
Oh no!

# Finn escapes

FN-2187 is a stormtrooper.
He realizes that the First Order
is evil, and he doesn't want
to be part of it anymore.
He wants to run away.

FN-2187 rescues Poe, and they
escape together. Poe thinks
that FN-2187 is a silly name,
so he renames his new friend
Finn. That's much better!

Poe and Finn steal a TIE fighter and try to fly away, but their ship gets shot down and crashes on Jakku. Finn parachutes to safety, but when he lands he finds that Poe has vanished.

# Rey

Jakku was once a battlefield
in the war against the Empire.
There are wrecked starships
scattered across the planet.
Many scavengers have come
to Jakku to take what they
can from the wreckage.

This girl is one of those
scavengers. Her name is Rey.
She has lived alone on Jakku
for many years. Rey was left on
the planet as a child, and she
doesn't remember her family.

# Rey in the junkyard

Rey is very good at scavenging. She always finds valuable bits of technology. She takes them to Niima Outpost, which is the biggest town on Jakku.

At Niima Outpost Rey trades what she finds for food, but it is never enough and she is always hungry!

Rey is a genius with machinery.
She has built herself a speeder
out of spare pieces of junk.

# Rescuing BB-8

Rey is relaxing and eating some food when she hears frightened beeping. It's BB-8! He is being kidnapped by another scavenger.

Even though Rey doesn't know BB-8, she leaps into action and rescues him. Good job, Rey!

BB-8 wants to stay with Rey,
but Rey offers to take him to
Niima Outpost instead.

# Unkar Plutt

Rey's boss is a mean junk dealer named Unkar Plutt. Unkar contro all of the food in Niima Outpost.

If the scavengers that work for Unkar can't find anything to trade, then they go hungry.

When Rey arrives at Niima, Unkar tries to buy BB-8 from her. Rey says no, and Unkar sends his gang of thugs after them. Luckily, Rey knows how to defend herself.

# Niima Outpost

After his TIE fighter crashes, Finn has to walk through the hot Jakku desert. Eventually he reaches Niima Outpost. Rey and BB-8 have defeated Unkar's thugs, but First Order stormtroopers are coming after them!

Rey and BB-8 run into Finn as they try to get away. They decide to join forces and escape together.

They need a ship to escape on. Rey finds a rusty old freighter underneath a tarp. It is called the *Millennium Falcon*.

# Battle above Jakku

Rey, Finn, and BB-8 take off in
the *Millennium Falcon*, but First
Order ships chase after them!

Rey is a great pilot. She manages
to outfly the First Order pilots.

Finn gets into the gunner
position and tries to destroy
the enemy ships.

Together they escape from Jakku,
but then the *Millennium Falcon*
breaks down.

# Han and Chewbacca

Han and his copilot, Chewbacca, are smugglers. Han used to own the *Millennium Falcon.*

The two smugglers are traveling in a huge star freighter. They come across their old ship broken down in space. They are very happy to have the *Millennium Falcon* back!

Han and Chewie are very famous. They helped the rebels win their war against the Empire. Rey and Finn are shocked when they realize who Han and Chewie are.

# Gangsters

Han and Chewie have made
a lot of enemies over the years.
One of these enemies is a gang of
pirates known as the Kanjiklub.

The Kanijiklub is a scruffy
group of thieves and bandits.
They are led by a fierce
warrior named Tasu Leech.

The Kanjiklub attack Han and
Chewie's freighter, but Han,
Chewie, Rey, Finn, and BB-8 all
escape in the *Millennium Falcon*.

# Rey is captured!

The band of brave heroes travel to visit an old friend of Han and Chewie's. Her name is Maz. She is one of the most famous smugglers in the galaxy.

Unfortunately, the First Order has tracked the heroes to Maz's castle.

An army of stormtroopers
lands to try to capture them.
There is a big battle, but Poe
and the Resistance arrive and
save the day! The stormtroopers
retreat, but they capture Rey
and take her away.

# The Resistance base

Han, Chewie, Finn, and BB-8 travel to the Resistance's secret base. They have learned that the First Order has built a giant weapon named the Starkiller on an icy planet. This is where Rey is being held prisoner.

At their base the Resistance puts together a plan to rescue Rey and destroy the Starkiller.

Han, Chewie, and Finn will sneak into the First Order base while Poe and his brave Resistance pilots attack from above.

# The Starkiller

Han, Finn, and Chewie land
on the Starkiller base in the
*Millennium Falcon*. At the same
time, Rey escapes from her
prison cell. They all find each
other inside the base.

They find out that there is
a problem. The Resistance's
X-wings can't shoot through
the Starkiller's thick armor.
What are they going to do?

# Battle in the base

The stormtroopers protecting
the Starkiller wear special
armor to keep themselves warm.
They are called snowtroopers.

The door into the Starkiller
is locked and guarded.
Finn and Rey need to
find a way to open it.

While Han and Chewie
defeat the troopers guarding
the door, Rey finds the box
that controls it.

Rey is able to open the door,
and Han and Chewie rush inside.
They place their explosives and
then Chewie sets them off.

# Poe into action

In the sky above the Starkiller, a big battle is raging. The X-wings of the Resistance are battling the TIE fighters of the First Order.

When Chewie sets off his explosives, it makes a hole in the Starkiller's armor.

Poe sees his chance! He fires
into the hole and soon the
Starkiller is badly damaged.
It starts to tear itself apart.

# Kylo's revenge

Kylo Ren is very angry. He storms
out into the snow looking for
Finn and Rey. Kylo doesn't
know that Finn and Rey are
stronger than he thinks.

Finn and Rey battle Kylo Ren.
It looks like Kylo is going to win,
but then something amazing
happens. He is defeated!

General Hux uses a shuttle to
rescue Kylo, while Finn and Rey
are picked up by Chewie in the
*Millennium Falcon.* The Starkiller
blows up as they fly to safety.

The Starkiller has been
destroyed. The Resistance
has won the battle, but the
war is only beginning!

# Quiz

1. What is the name of the First Order's Supreme Leader?

2. Who created the Resistance?

3. What is the name of Poe's droid?

4. Which planet does Rey live on?

5. Which ship do Rey and Finn use to escape from Jakku?

6. Who is Han Solo's copilot?

7. What is the name of the First Order's secret weapon?

8. What are the First Order's cold-weather soldiers known as?

**Answers on page 47**

# Glossary

**Droid**
A type of robot

**Freighter**
A ship that transports cargo

**Scavenger**
Someone who searches through worthless junk to find useful things

**Starkiller**
A giant secret weapon built by the First Order

**Starship**
A vehicle used to travel through space

**Track**
To follow something or someone

**Technology**
Machinery and equipment made using scientific knowledge

# Index

Answers to the quiz on pages 44 and 45:
1. Snoke  2. Princess Leia  3. BB-8  4. Jakku
5. The *Millennium Falcon*  6. Chewbacca
7. The Starkiller  8. snowtroopers

# Have you read these other great books from DK?

## BEGINNING TO READ ALONE ②

Join Han Solo on his exciting adventures across the galaxy.

Join Luke Skywalker and the rebels as they battle the evil Empire.

Discover a LEGO® *Star Wars™* galaxy on the brink of war.

## READING ALONE ③

Take a look inside the Empire's deadliest weapon, if you dare!

Luke Skywalker is the last Jedi. Can he help the rebels win the war?

Learn all about Yoda's battles and how he uses the Force.